Shtf

Survival

The Skills and Mindset to Survive When the World Collapses

(The Prepper's Guide to Food and Water Storage for Disaster Preparedness)

Jeffrey Doak

Published By **Bella Frost**

Jeffrey Doak

Shtf Survival: The Skills and Mindset to Survive When the World Collapses (The Prepper's Guide to Food and Water Storage for Disaster Preparedness)

ISBN   978-1-77485-952-0

No part of this guidebook shall be reproduced in any form without permission in writing from the publisher except in the case of brief quotations embodied in critical articles or reviews.

Legal & Disclaimer

The information contained in this ebook is not designed to replace or take the place of any form of medicine or professional medical advice. The information in this ebook has been provided for educational & entertainment purposes only.

The information contained in this book has been compiled from sources deemed reliable, and it is accurate to the best of the Author's knowledge; however, the Author cannot guarantee its accuracy and validity and cannot be held liable for any errors or omissions. Changes are periodically made to this book. You must consult your doctor or get professional medical advice before using any of the suggested remedies, techniques, or information in this book.

Table of contents

Chapter 1: How To Deal With The
Aftermath Of Disasters 1

Chapter 2: What Do You Do After An
Emergency? 11

Chapter 3: How To Repair Your House ... 24

Chapter 4: How Can You Repair Your
Finances 33

Chapter 5: Tips To Help You Deal With The
Direct Aftermath 42

Chapter 6: Food Preparation, Food Items
.... 45

Chapter 7: Medical Supplies 76

Chapter 8: Survival Items 94

Chapter 9: Hunting, Gathering And Self
Defense 108

Chapter 10: Miscellaneous Items 121

Chapter 11: Planning Short, Medium &
Long Term 126

Chapter 12: How To Store Water More Effectively 138

Chapter 13: How To Store Food More Efficiently 143

Chapter 14: Preserving Your Fresh Food 156

Chapter 15: How To Replenish Your Food In A Survival Situation 161

Chapter 16: What Is An Electromagnetic Pulse? 165

Chapter 17: The Worst Case Scenario .. 173

Chapter 18: Surviving 181

Chapter 1: How to deal with the aftermath of disasters

But suddenly, you are faced with the impossible. What's your next move

Many prepper's and survival specialists spend hours discussing how crucial it is to prepare for disaster and what steps we should take to ensure our family is prepared. But, nobody really discusses what happens after the disaster is over. It is true that there are not many people who concentrate on the aftermath. Instead, they focus on the prepping aspect. While the preparation aspect is still vital, it's important to also focus on the aftermath.

Many people have a plan but do not know what to do once the emergency has passed. It puts them in danger unknowingly. It is difficult to know how each individual will be affected. There may be times when the effect is subtle and others that are more severe. However, it is crucial to look at the aftermath. It doesn't really matter if the danger has passed, because you still have to be at risk.

You aren't alone in a dangerous situation. The outcome of the situation will depend on how you react to it and how you handle it.

A terrible disaster can cause devastating effects. A person can experience stress, anxiety, confusions, shock, sadness and other emotions. These emotions can be overwhelming but necessary in order to give yourself and those around your the chance to rebuild.

Get in touch with your emotions to heal and open the door for you to feel better

Even if it seems like everything is gone, you don't need to let disasters or emergencies define you. When disaster strikes, there is always hope. Your life can be rebuilt from the ground up. You will feel overwhelmed by emotions and instincts. Don't fight them.

If you can begin to see the whole picture and be open to your emotions, it will allow you to heal. This will help you get back on your feet, emotionally and physically. Remember this, it is the natural healing process. While thousands will claim that this is complete rubbish and that emotions only cause people to do crazy stuff, it's your emotions who will allow to you move on from the pain and rebuild your life.

It's bad to store emotions, no matter how strong or weak they might be. They'll just come out at the wrong moments. This is not what your body wants. Anger will soon turn to anger and it will be directed towards the wrong person. Instead, allow your emotions to flow. It is not good for your health and also it isn't good for the mind.

You must first grieve. If you have lost someone dear, it will be a difficult and lengthy process.

Although everyone grieves their loss in their own unique ways, it is possible to allow yourself to grieve and let the healing process begin. But, you don't have to mourn the loss of a loved one or friend to grieve. It is important to grieve if the family home was lost.

You must also take good care of yourself. This doesn't necessarily mean getting medical attention. But it does include things like proper nutrition and adequate sleep. Perhaps you will find it easier to express your emotions if you can find a way to do so. You don't have to resort to drugs or alcohol. Instead, find an outlet where you can express yourself.

Don't rush into making major decisions. It takes time to get back on your feet. You should take your time to examine any matter presented to you. Clearing your mind can help you make informed decisions.

Let's face it, the past is what it is. Although it may seem harsh to tell you to forget about it, it actually makes it easier. You can forget about the past and focus on what happened. The guilt will always be there and it will really hurt you. The guilt will not help you rebuild your life.

You can talk it out with your friends and family. It's important that you sit down and talk about how you feel to those close to you. It is possible to talk about your feelings, as well as how you felt. Keep telling yourself you can make it through this because you can.

Anybody can survive a disaster. Even if there has been a significant loss, it is possible to recover. You can take it slow, and just take small steps to rebuild your life. It won't always be easy to cope with the emotions that follow a disaster. However, this doesn't necessarily mean you cannot overcome them.

How to deal with Emergencies

It is important to understand that emergency situations can take time to heal. But, when you learn how to handle them, you'll be able make the transition easier. There are many easy and good ways to help. One way is to recognize when things become too difficult.

No one likes to admit that they are feeling under pressure. However, it's okay to need help. Do not think that you are weak for seeking help. Get help if you need it. You should take a deep breath and stop worrying if things are getting too stressful.

Talking is an important tool to aid others. Talking is an excellent way to express your emotions. You can put things in perspective by letting go of all your anger. This will help you have a clearer mental picture. When you are done with negative thoughts, you can start to find practical ways of dealing with them and even conquer them.

To help you deal with the situation, it is a good idea for professionals to assist you. Although it doesn't necessarily signify weakness, it does mean you may struggle to understand or express emotions. It might be worth seeking professional guidance to help you get past the difficulties.

Take Care of Your Family and Friends

Do not forget that your children and younger siblings will also find the situation stressful. Although your primary concern is the children, don't forget about their feelings. Sometimes they just need a little bit of encouragement and reassurance to feel safe.

This should be repeated to all members of the family, no matter their age. Even the smallest encouragement can make a difference in helping children feel safe. You don't have to be scared of your children.

Plan of Action

Plan of action is one of the most powerful tools you can have to deal with the aftermath after a disaster. Because it is impossible to predict how the devastation will unfold, you cannot plan this before it happens. However, assess the situation quickly and decide on the next steps.

Be clear about what you want, how you are going to do it and what is required. It is essential to assess both the financial situation and the physical condition of your home. It doesn't necessarily have to be well-thought out. A basic plan of three steps is sufficient to get you started. A little plan will help you cope with the aftermath and avoid panicking.

There's nothing to be afraid of in the aftermath

The worst and most terrifying moments of your life will come when an emergency occurs. Even if you have done serious prepping, you don't know what could happen. But you can make sure you are safe. What comes next can be just the same as the actual disaster, because so many things are unknown.

Floods and terrorist attacks are both scary. Fear can make you resentful and keep you from moving forward. It is true that it can be scary to deal with the aftermath of a natural or man-made disaster. But don't let this stop you from moving forward. You've done the hard part. Now take control and rebuild.

Chapter 2: What Do You Do After an Emergency?

Staying Safe in the Instant Aftermath

When disaster strikes, chaos ensues quickly. However, it continues even after the event is over. The outcome of your family's destiny could depend on your first decisions. But losing your head only makes matters worse. Safety is essential in the immediate aftermath of any disaster. However, there are simple ways you can stay safe.

It is important to first check the area around you. If the disaster was severe enough, you may lose half the street and be unable to return. If that's the case, then you need to evacuate to designated safe zones. Because everyone is in a panic, it can be difficult for you to tell the truth. It may also prove difficult to communicate with anyone via telephone. Check the local news, on radio or television, to determine if anyone is warning citizens to leave.

There might be emergency teams like the National Guard and local emergency service that help people reach safe areas in the most affected areas. Follow the instructions provided to ensure you and others are able move away from danger zones and to reach safe areas. Although there will be panic and some people may want to stay put, it is best to move away from the danger zone. Avoid residing in an area that is not safe.

If you are concerned about chemical or biological dangers, please follow the instructions issued by the government. As you move around, be mindful of falling debris as they could cause injuries. This is not the best thing to do in case of a natural or terrorist disaster. The immediate area may not be safe and you need to evacuate your family quickly and calmly.

Don't worry, there will be safe zones that will look out for everyone. There could be additional danger from another storm, another attack. When there is, you need to forget about your house and work, and just go with your family. You don't want to be delayed or waste time if there is a threat.

Once you've decided whether the area should be kept, you will need to treat any injuries. If you are injured, you should seek out medical attention. It doesn't matter if the injuries don't appear serious but it's a smart thing to have a professional examine you. There are many things you can do to help shock victims.

Minor cuts, scrapes, or bruises can be treated at home. You can also use bandages to keep them from getting worse until you seek medical attention. A splint may be necessary for broken bones. It doesn't really matter if someone is hurt, but you must ensure that they are awake and talking.

Sometimes, you might have to manage medical issues on your own for several days before a doctor is available. If you find yourself in an area without access to emergency help, then it may be a long wait.

The hospital will be able to treat serious injuries. These cases are critical and should be taken seriously. You can help the patient by talking to them and cleaning their wounds using anti-germ soaps. Cover any open wounds with a bandage.

Sterile and medical bandages are often used to prevent dirt and germs from entering wounds. To avoid infections and contamination, bandages need to be changed every few days. It can be stressful. However, try not to panic.

Beware of Aftershocks & Renewed Dangers

Your area may be affected by major earthquakes and storms. There are always seconds. A major storm can bring about minor storms, with torrential rain and flash floods. Because of their unpredictable nature, aftershocks may prove just as dangerous and deadly as earthquakes. Renewing dangers and aftershocks are always possible, so be mindful of any potential problems in these days.

You, and everyone else, must remain calm. It's not an easy task but it's essential. Remain calm and make a decision.

You must be able to handle the situation and guide your family to safety. If your home is unsafe, you must move the family to another location. This can be done with someone you know, a relative, or a friend of the family who wasn't affected by the catastrophe. However you should ensure that you travel to a safe area. If you are still able to access the television, please listen to the advice and offer your assistance to others.

There will be many others who are in a worse position than you. If you can help, please do. Before you go, ensure that your family is safe. However, there is no absolute rule saying you must help a neighbor or friend. Your personal decision.

Be aware that if you leave home, you must only return when it is advised. This can be a lengthy wait, but it is worth it. Make sure you have a clear understanding of the situation before you return.

However, you are one of your greatest risks in the immediate aftermath to a disaster. You can do some of the most crazy things, like using the electricity. It may seem innocent to turn on the light or TV, but it can be very dangerous. When your home or business has suffered water damage or flooding, it is important that you think before you act.

If you live in flood-prone areas, it is best to remain put and stay inside. Your first instinct might be for you to get out, but if the water level is rising you may find yourself trapped in your car. Let's be real, you don't want to be trapped on low-level ground any time of the day, even if your ability to swim.

To prevent the water from getting in, it is best to lock all windows and doors. Call the emergency services once you have done this to get assistance so you know exactly what to do. Sometimes, fire and rescue crews have boats and may be able to help you. Flood water rises rapidly so it's important to be prepared.

It's best to stay out of the water after the flood, as it can be full with germs, dirt, and debris. If you can't evacuate your home immediately, it is best to keep the family out of the water. This is something that most people are aware of, but your mind can be faulty in difficult situations. Avoid ditches, drains, and ponds when you venture out in ankle-deep water.

Allowing family members to know that you are safe

It doesn't matter whether you've been separated from your family during an emergency or not. You must also let them know that you're OK. If your home or landlines have been damaged, it might prove difficult to relay this information. Your cell phone is a better option. You'll hopefully be able to communicate with the family.

Sometimes, it takes a while for the lines to open. Don't panic though; eventually you'll be able to. You can send texts letting people know that you are fine and that you will contact you when possible. If your cell phone is not working, you might try to use an old-fashioned pager or beeper. Even if your power isn't out yet, there is still a chance you could use the computer to send an email telling everyone where you are and that everything is fine.

While it's better to contact your family directly, it's not always possible. You may need to contact Red Cross when this is not an option. Red Cross and other charitable organisations are available to help you in times of disaster. They can be reached at their contact information and ask if you have any relatives who have passed through their teams. It may not always be possible to find them but you will at least know they are safe.

It can be hard to find missing family members. This can be difficult if you live in an area where everything has been destroyed or evacuated.

People helping with evacuations, like the National Guard, might be able provide some indication of their location. But in areas completely destroyed, it will be a nightmare. If possible, get help from the local catastrophe committee and see if any family members have checked into local hospitals, or with the Red Cross.

If you are searching for missing persons, it is possible that there will be no information for several weeks. In the case of mass destruction, everything is in order and it could take some time before families are reunited. Keep fighting for your family.

Take a look at the structure of you home

The storm could have caused damage to the home, making it unsuitable for habitation. To assess whether your home is safe to return to, it's important to conduct basic home checks. The street may have been deemed safe, but it does not guarantee that the home will be completely safe.

You should only return to your home after you are told that it is safe. Even if you were in a safe place when the disaster occurred, this is a different situation. You still need to be careful and inspect your home.

First, examine the exterior condition and structure of the home. Look out for signs such as roof cracks or instability. You should also ensure that there are no power lines within the area. Additionally, you should look out for signs like gas leaks or structural damages.

Most often, problems found on the outside are a sign of more serious problems within the home. You might be safer calling a fire inspector or a home inspection first. It's impossible to know what condition your home will be in after a hurricane. You might be able to build a home that is sturdy and beautiful, but it could still suffer severe damage. If you are lucky enough, you may only have minor repairs. It does vary depending on each disaster or emergency situation.

Take a look at the utilities available in your home

After you have assessed the property's shape, it's now time to determine if all utilities are working properly. Before you can return to your home fulltime, it is essential that heating, electrical, as well as plumbing systems, are in top condition. These are serious issues that should be addressed quickly, but accurately!

For safety reasons, you should turn off any exterior shut-off points that supply electricity or gas. If not, you can switch off the power at home. Check for frayed wires or loose wires. This could indicate a problem in the electricity. Also, the circuit box should be checked because it is possible that there has been internal damage. Call an electrician to make sure your home has safe electrical supply and repair any damage.

If the street has experienced problems with its plumbing, it is likely that you will too. To avoid problems with your water supply, you should not use any sinks, bathtubs, or showers. Even if there's only the slightest issue with the sewage system, your home may be affected in many different ways.

Chapter 3: How to Repair Your House

Your home is a very important aspect of your life. But, if it's damaged by a natural disaster, it could become a wreck. It can be difficult for a homeowner to rebuild their home after a disaster. However, you don't need to despair. Your home can be rebuilt even if it is damaged by flooding, an accident, a terror attack, or other causes.

You can assess the damage and know if the home is safe.

First, assess the entire home. First, take a look at the exterior. Check for signs of damage to foundations, support walls, and entry points. It is a good idea take photographs and make notes of everything you see so that you have a complete picture.

It is not wise to climb up to the roof and inspect it. However, you should take notes from where you are. Although you might be able to call a home inspector to approve the building, it might not be feasible right away. Although some gasses can be hard to detect, you should immediately report any suspicions or hearing hissing noises. The most obvious sign that gas is escaping from somewhere is hissing noises. For propane tanks, locate the shutoff points and close them to stop the gas from escaping.

Also, look out for damage to power lines or cables entering the home. Additionally, search for signs that gas problems may be present. There are many indicators that your home is in danger of structural damage. Call the professionals immediately if you notice any. If the exterior is causing significant damage, it is likely that the interior will be as well. This is why it is best not to enter the property. It is best to call in a home inspector first to verify the stability of your home. Only then, can you enter the home.

If you suspect that there may be a gas leak in your home, it is best to get away as soon as possible. Do not stop to retrieve any belongings. The fire department will be able help with shutting off the gas and making sure the home is safe.

Avoid forcing doors and windows that are jammed to the ground. It can prove fatal. The doors might be supporting parts of the home. You should not force them to open. This could lead to serious damage and make you very unsafe. You can get to the property via the front door but not the garage door or the back door.

Step into the Home

If you do decide to enter your home, it is possible that there are animal squatters. This can be as bothersome as human-squatters and can also prove difficult to handle. Unfortunately, there are many animals that seek shelter during severe weather.

Rodents, insects, and even snakes may seek shelter. You should be cautious. Use a stick to knock on the floors if possible. It will signal the animals that you are present and hopefully they will filter away.

If you suspect that there are infestations, call an exterminator to address the issue. To temporarily solve the problem, you can set traps for mice later, once your home is secured properly.

It is important to walk through the whole house, beginning in the hallway and ending at the basement. It is important to inspect each room thoroughly so that any damage can be identified and recorded. Some items may be unstable so be cautious where you stand, and what you touch. There are also potential for floor damage so be careful. The repairs may come later. Right now, your only focus should remain on the security of your home and establishing what repairs need to be made.

Most household objects can be saved. The items that you plan to keep should be placed on the side. Damaged items should be thrown out. To make it easy for the rubbish bin to collect them, place any broken or damaged household goods on the driveway. Sometimes furniture can still be saved if it is only slightly damaged. It might require minor repairs or polishing. For unstable furniture or items that are severely damaged, dispose of them.

Flooding is a sign that it is time to drain the water. With handheld pumps, pump out as much water you can. If the water is very large, use large generator pumps. If you live near an area subject to frequent flooding, then you might already have some equipment. Open the windows once the water has dried and dry the carpets, blankets, and covers. Although they may need to be cleaned, the main concern is drying them out.

You should also be cautious about floors that are too sagging or damaged.

Temporary Repairs are a Priority

Although there might be extensive repairs to the house, it is not necessary right now. You must get the home secured. This will mean making temporary or minor repairs. You will be able to make the minor repairs first, which will secure the home. However, the more serious repairs will need a later date when you can get the right contractors in to start the work.

You should first cover any holes in the walls. Board up broken windows, doors, and other points of entry that are not secure. Clean up all the clutter and broken objects in your home. If you're familiar with the process, replacing flooring or painting walls damaged can be done easily by you. You can do the most basic repairs first. The rest will be easy.

Call the gas and electric company as well as other major utility companies to make sure the systems work within your home and are safe.

Moving on to the Big Damage

Sometimes, major damage to a home won't be repaired for some time, or even months. But it is crucial to get the repairs done. Major repairs are difficult to make yourself unless the homeowner is a professional builder.

If you don't have the experience to handle major tasks such as replacing support walls and reconnecting the water supply, it can be very difficult. Contractors are needed to complete major tasks such as replacing supporting walls or replacing a significant portion of the home. But, before you sign any deals, make sure to not pay upfront.

While this is expensive, you should still consider it if possible. In the meantime you will need to find alternate shelter until your home is safe and habitable. Keep receipts and verify your insurance policy if you intend to move until the work is completed.

Take photos of the damage to be able to prove your claim. You should also keep receipts, estimates, and checks related to the work.

Your Home Is Important, but Don't Give Up!

Your home is the only thing you can trust in these difficult times. But you should be aware of the risks. There might be serious issues within your home. If you don't know what to do, you could end up in serious harm's way. Make sure you take all precautions and are safe. Ask the gas or electricity companies for a second opinion and ensure your safety.

Chapter 4: How can you repair your finances

A disaster can leave you feeling stressed and under pressure. Although the majority of disasters result in a drop in family finances, there are still ways you can assess the situation and make repairs.

Analyse your financial situation

First, it is essential to examine your finances from every angle and identify your financial problems. Look closely at your bank statements to find out what savings you have and how much property repair will cost. The amount of money that you have lost already from the disaster is another thing to consider.

If you are a home-based business or small, you will need to estimate the total loss of clients, business property, materials, and how much it will cost to reopen the business. While this may seem daunting, you should be able to give an estimate so that you are aware of any financial issues. It is possible to estimate the cost of renting a smaller office in downtown if it was damaged. You also need to calculate how much it will cost you to replace your company property. The same applies for the home.

If the business has been completely wiped out and stock has been lost, it can cost you a substantial amount of money in order to replace it. So get your proof of the loss and contact your insurance company as soon as possible. These are the people who will help you to go through your financial statements thoroughly and don't be afraid of using their services.

The best thing is to visit a free financial consultant to find out your current situation. The counselor can usually review all bills and each penny to determine if there is any money that has been lost or gone out.

Make your next move

There are many options, and some of them may be very beneficial to you. It is important to discuss your options with a financial professional and the family about your next steps. You can also talk about how you can restore some credit. Check your credit score, and also obtain a copy. This will allow you to assess the current credit standing. It will take very little time for the damage to be apparent.

Next, make sure creditors are aware of your situation. In most cases lenders will be happy to grant a little extra time to help those who are experiencing financial hardships or other serious financial problems, particularly after a major event. While some companies might not be able to extend payments, others will appreciate your situation.

It would be a good idea to write an honest and complete letter to all creditors explaining the situation.

This will prove that you are willing to repay the debts, but not able due to the current crisis. You can request a delay in late payments.

Importantly, however, you cannot stop paying any type of debt. If you are truly in trouble, reduce the amount of payments made to creditors to the minimum. Paying in arrears can damage credit scores. If you cannot afford to make the minimum payments, then return any items still being paid for such as sofas, televisions, or cars. While this won't make your credit look great, it won't cause any major damage to it.

If you feel it is possible, speak to creditors and set up a payment schedule for the foreseeable future. This will include explaining the situation and telling them what you can afford. Even if the amount is lower, many companies will accept payment. While it isn't a guarantee, it may help you to keep your credit score from being damaged. Remember, nothing is worse than anything.

Sometimes you can get a six-month break or relief from paying your mortgage. It can vary between mortgage companies, but some offer this option. You will need to ask and if they give you this option, at least six month to get yourself back on track and hopefully all financial worries will be forgotten.

You should avoid filing bankruptcy. Your credit rating will be destroyed. Your credit will go down the drain faster than any other financial institution and it will be difficult to reestablish your financial standing. You may need to consult a financial adviser if you have lost a lot of money due to the disaster. A consolidation lawyer can help you reduce debt payments to put your finances in a better financial place.

But, if you're unable or unwilling to work for any reason, you can apply to welfare. Even if it isn't enough to support your family, you may be able to contact the welfare office and request help. You may be eligible for an aid loan or emergency loan if you can prove the severity of your situation. Again, this depends on your specific circumstances.

Rebuilding and Reestablishing Credit

You should know your incoming monies and your outgoing funds. Knowing your overheads is essential to understanding your financial situation. You need to look at the bank statements closely.

This means you must know the monthly costs of your rent, gas or electricity, and any other utility costs. A list of your weekly expenses for food and life, car, insurance, home, contents, and health should be made. Every debt and every bill must be listed, including school fees and child-care costs.

Once you've accounted for every penny going into and out your home, you can start to think about ways you can save. It is possible for your finances to take a huge hit. You must find ways to save money. This might mean reducing grocery costs, or even getting rid of cable TV. When you're willing to do the work, savings can be made at any cost. You can put the money you save towards an emergency fund and funds to fix your home.

Next, make a budget. Make sure you stick to it. This means you have to be very strict in all areas of expenses. Even though you won't be able to spend a lot, even if it's for a few weeks, it will pay off in the long-term. All your savings can go into an emergency savings account.

You can rebuild your finances by having a little money saved up. This will allow you to have a backup plan in case of emergency. Even five dollars per month can be worthwhile.

But, rebuilding credit after a hard hit can take time. It is possible to get a credit card that allows you to make small purchases. You could purchase a television for 90 dollars, and then each week pay the bills and make payments. You can do this with a few small-priced items. This will slowly build up a track record of consistent payments, which is great for credit.

Credit cards can also be used to build credit but can be risky, especially if you have poor finances. It might be worth considering avoiding credit cards for the time being.

Chapter 5: Tips To Help You Deal With the Direct Aftermath

It doesn't matter if it is a minor flood or a major terrorist act, emergencies and disasters can be very unpleasant. But there will be lots of confusion. You can't fall for the trap of feeling afraid or let the situation ruin you.

Here are some quick tips to recall important information.

Find a Safe Location

You may feel safe, but the danger has passed. If you don't have shelter at home, you should seek it. It's impossible to predict the future so make sure you have shelter. You must go to the hospital immediately if you are injured.

Keep in mind that there can be panic out there.

Shock is a natural reaction, so don't fight it

Acceptance is key to rebuilding a life after suffering from a disaster. You can't change the past. It will be impossible to live each day over again. This will not happen in minutes or days. It might take months or longer.

When medical attention is needed, get it

You should not rush to the hospital if you have a tiny cut. It's okay to go to the doctor to check your health. However, if you don't have any bleeding, you will only be hindering your recovery. Although everyone rushes for help when disaster strikes, this can lead to long delays and panic. It's hard for us to know, but we can predict that the most urgent patients will be our first priority.

If you are feeling well, but still want to be checked up on, visit your local client or doctor. You can get help for many injuries from doctors who are available to you at your local hospital.

Help Wherever You Can

This is not an easy task, but it may be possible to help those who are less fortunate if your situation is somewhat dire. This does not mean rescuing people from apartment blocks. It just means looking out for their neighbors to find out if any need and securing their home. It's the little things that make a difference.

Chapter 6: Food Preparation, Food Items

Food Preserving Tools, Bottles and Rings for Pressure Canners

Canning and bottled food are great if you don't have a lot of time to restore order. But what happens if you run low? There is a limit to the amount of meat that you can freeze. This will cause strain on any other preparations that require freezing. The same is true for dried meat. It is important to have more options for long periods of time.

There are very few options for you at any extreme of the world. You have only limited options.

There are many options, each with their own risks. You run the risk that you will be exposed to any future events and expose yourself to others. You will be able to save as much meat as possible if you have the funds. This will allow you to limit your trips and reduce the risk of being hurt.

You will be able store any meat, beef, pork, or chicken you hunt if you have the proper equipment such pressure canners and bottlers.

Below is a brief overview on how to preserve and preserve meat.

The best thing about bottled meat is that it comes pre-cooked and can be used whenever you wish. The shelf life is typically 3+years.

Step One

You should cut the meat into small cubes. You don't even have to cut them. Just make sure they are all roughly the same size. You can trim the fat or gristle but most will cook off.

Step Two

You will need to put a few inches water in the bottom (not a hot bath) of your pressure canner. Once that is done, you can turn it up to high. To heat the bottles, make sure you have hot water in a separate pan on the stove. This prevents bottles from getting distorted later and also allows water to escape.

Step 3

Put your meat in sterilized and clean containers.

Step Four

In each bottle, you will need to put approximately half a teaspoon or more salt.

Step Five

Now fill the jars and boil the water. You will need to open the bottles until they reach the neck. Then, you'll want to use a knife or a fork to remove any trapped air bubbles. The more air you extract, the better your finished product. You can continue these two steps until the water level is perfect and all air is gone.

Step Six

Simply screw on all the rings and lids to your bottles, and then put them into your canner. You can place the lid on the pressure cooker and heat it to 12lbs. Keep it at 12 lbs pressure for at most 55 minutes. Monitor it carefully to make sure it doesn't drop low or get too hot. Once the 55 minutes are up, you can turn off your cooker and let it cool down.

By stacking your bottles you can double how many you can preserve at once. It also makes it faster to process large amounts of food. To make it easier, begin small for your first few batches. You can also leave your bottles in the pressurecanner to cool overnight if you do it right before you go to bed.

Food Preparation Tools. Cooking Utensils. Eating Utensils. Pans.

Only one set of high-quality, quality eating utensils will be required if you are on the move with someone else or yourself. It is important to consider both space and weight when carrying equipment.

Vargo's collection of cutlery was a constant pick when I searched for high-quality kitchen utensils. Vargo's range of cutlery is versatile and can be found HERE.

If you have a safe place to hide, like a bunker or protected home, you will have much more space. A cheaper set of cooking utensils could be used.

You can use pots and skillets with gas stoves. But if you cook on open fires, good pots or pans are essential. Cast iron pots or pans have a major problem. If you have had to carry them for any length, it is likely that you will end up throwing them into the river. They can withstand being scratched and dented, thrown into fires, and all other abuses. But you want to avoid them.

Vargo has created some pretty good titanium cookware. Both pots and pans are lighter than either stainless steel or aluminium.

It is essential that all of your cooking utensils are built to last. There won't be any shop left open in case of an emergency. You will not need to leave your house if you can't cook. Aim to have at most two to three of every kitchen item. A good knife is essential as well as any tools you will be using frequently in the kitchen. Plates, bowls, every item in your kitchen that you use, you need to keep track of.

You should have one good-sized plate and one large bowl for any situation, whether you are driving or walking. To determine if the items you own are useful, go camping and take them with you. It is not worth having all the necessary equipment in case of an emergency. But if something does happen, they will be more than adequate.

Bottle Openers and Can-Openers

Although you might not be carrying much canned goods when on the road, it is a good idea to have some handy in case you need them. You need a small, reliable and high-quality opener. Best Glide makes can openers of military quality that are built in the USA. They will last for years.

You will need a large supply of canned goods if you live in a bunker. As wear and tear can cause can openers to become insufficient, it's a good idea to have several.

This P-38 can opening tool was created for military personnel. It can be used with any size can. The P-51 can be used in place of the P-38. They are both very affordable at just a few dollars. Visit HERE to order them and receive a complete set instructions.

It is also important to have a bottle opener, because you never know what you might need.

MREs and Tinned Food

In an emergency situation you will need food. MREs are Meals Ready to Eat. You only have so many food cans and packets you can carry. They can be used to make a variety meals, as well as include other goodies and accessories. They have a very long shelf life, so you can take them with you wherever you go.

If you plan to keep your MREs for a long time, more variety is better. If you have the space, it is possible to stock a greater variety of MREs as well as Backpacker Meals.

MREs are thought to be the same as Backpackers Meals, even though many haven't tried them. MREs are often considered to be superior to Backpacking Meals.

* Being constantly on the move, and making the most of what you have, means that your calorie count can really matter. Although backpacker meals are typically

400-600 calories, most military MREs have close to 1250 calories.

* You will usually receive the main meal and a side like fruit, rice or vegetables with every MRE. Variety is the key to a happy life.

* Along with the main dish, side dish, and MRE, you will often get bread and crackers to go with your meal. Unless you order additional sides, most backpacking meals consist of one main dish.

* MREs often include a dessert, and sometimes even chocolate. These are all the things you won't find on a normal backpacking dinner.

MREs may be eaten either hot or cold. MREs are also available cold. This is a good option for those who are constantly on the go or don't have enough time to heat a fire. They will be more delicious hot but sometimes it's better to have a cold meal.

* With every MRE, you get a drink combination. This mix can be used to make tea, coffee, hot cocoa, or a shake.

* Every MRE comes with various accessories. There are many things you can buy, such as matches, spoons and gum, toothpicks, Tabasco sauce salt, pepper, Tabasco sugar, Tabasco sauce and Tabasco paste.

* MREs come equipped with a flameless heating device that can be used to heat your MRE in the cold or wind.

Bottled water or stored water

An average person needs at least one gallon per day. On foot, there will be only one or two days supply. It is essential to have enough water treatment tablets or liquid on hand in order to boil any water you are able to obtain. Water taps are not always available for you to refill your water as you travel. I will detail water treatment options more in depth later.

You have the possibility to store even more water when you build a bunker. A water tank can be installed under your home to store rainwater. If you plan to store water for a long period of time, you should make sure it is treated so it doesn't become contaminated.

Food storage in cans

Cans are great if there are people you want to bug in on, but if you don't then you'll regret taking along cans of food. MREs provide you with more space and weight options if you are either on foot or riding in a car.

It is best if you only store the basics. The more you accumulate, the more you can branch out to luxury items and/or other items to diversify the items you have. It's not necessary to purchase a whole year's worth of stuff in one week. Just start with a handful each month.

It is important that you replace food items when they are no longer needed. It is crucial to maintain a master listing of what you have and how much, as well as when it is due to expire.

Next, I will share a top ten list with you of the best foods for bugging.

Rice

A bag is a great idea if you see rice at a special price, especially when it is in large bulk quantities. If it isn't on special, don't worry about it. You can always double the quantity next time. Rice can be kept in a dry place for as long as 10 years. Rice will give you a large boost in carbohydrates.

Beans

Beans are rich in protein and one of your best money-saving survival foods. When stored correctly, dried beans can keep for up to ten more years. To preserve the oxygen in the container, they should be stored in a food safe container.

Cornmeal

Cornmeal can be stored longer, giving you more oil and carbohydrates. It can be stored almost as long as the beans if it is kept the same way. Cornmeal is more easy to use than other flours.

Lard

Lard is a more versatile oil than any other and offers a higher number of calories. Lard can last longer when kept in a dark, cool place.

Salt

Salt is an essential survival tool. You can use salt to cook meats, season your meals, store food, and as a barter. Salt can be stored in a cool and dark place for a long time.

Canned Vegetables & Fruits

Although canned tomatoes and acidic fruits are less durable than canned vegetables, they should still be stored in your pantry. You can store canned goods you don't eat in sealed containers so that they can be rotated before expiring. You can store most canned goods for at least five years if they are not being used.

Canned Meats

Canned meats are an excellent option when you need to stock a home or bunker. Canned meats like chicken, tuna and ham can be stored for up to ten-years.

Sugar & Honey

Sugar and honey are great options to add calories and flavor in post-disaster settings. Honey can last for years if stored in a cool, dry place. Both are useful for bartering as they can be stored and stored in large quantities.

Pastas

Pasta won't keep as long as rice. However, it will last at least five years when stored correctly. Pasta is also a large space-hogger, so be aware of this. Although it takes up a lot more space, pasta is much lighter.

Peanut Butter

This peanut butter is a great source for fat, calories, protein and you will be glad that you have it. Peanut butter will last up to five years, if stored in a cool and dark place.

Storage

It is easy to store beans, cornmeal, rice, sugar and pasta in large five-gallon storage containers. In a large, sealable bucket, place about 1 cup of salt into a baggie. You can then add whatever food you want to keep in there on top until the bucket fills up. After sealing the bucket, place a few ounces on top. This will help to remove oxygen from the bucket.

Sugar, Tea and Coffee

These are just a few of the things I mentioned. But I felt that they merited a section of their own! You should only buy granulated and powdered sugar. Avoid sugars in paper bags. They won't keep out dampness, so insects and other animals could chew through them. Avoid sugars that are in plastic bags. If you do re-bag your sugar, be sure to include a label and date.

It is a great idea to stockpile coffee and tea. They are also great for keeping you awake on long nights, and during sentry duty. Even if your don't drink, you can guarantee they will be extremely useful later for bartering and trading.

Salt, Pepper and Herbs

We've covered salt before so I won't be writing much about it. Make sure you have it! Salt has a long shelf life. Store as much salt as possible and then double the amount. Keep it dry and out of reach of water.

The importance of pepper and herbs for preservation is not as great as salt. However, unless you are going to be eating the same food over and again, pepper and herbs will come in handy. They will eventually lose their effectiveness, but they can be stored in a cool, dry location

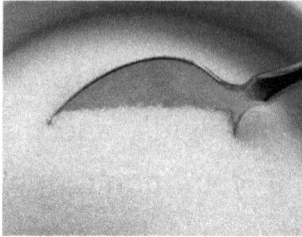

for many years.

Candy, Sweets, Chocolates

If you are in a survival situation, chocolate can help to lift your spirits. Dark chocolate is the most nutritious. The best way to store it is in bulk quantities of chips. To protect your chocolate from insects, store it in a bucket like other food products. Two years is a good time to store chocolate.

Hard candy makes a great addition for any preppers stockpile. It isn't very nutritious, but it can be used to barter or as a treat.

Consider adding some Nutella jars if you have the space. Nutella can make anything

taste good!

Dehydrated soup mix

A slow cooker or soup is a great way to enjoy meats that you've preserved or canned. You can either purchase readymade soup mixes from a store or make your own. These soup mixtures can last for between one to two years. They will also make preserved meat more delicious. Ready Nutrition provides the following recipes.

Vegetable Soup

* 1/3 Cup dried vegetable flakes (any combination such a tomatoes, onion and peas as well as celery, celery, carrots, celery, or zucchini)

* 1 TBL spoon bulgur Wheat

* 1 tablespoon small pasta

* 1/4 Tbsp dried sweet basil

1/4 Tbsp dried parsley

* 12 teaspoon onion powder and garlic powder

Salt and pepper to suit your taste

* 2 cups boiling hot water

Blend the dried vegetables in the blender until you get flakes. 1/3 cup. Reserve the rest for another day. 1/3 cup flaked vegetables can be put in a pint tin thermos. Add basil, garlic powder and onion powder. Season with salt and pepper. Bulgur wheat or pasta should be added to your thermos. Bring broth to boil. Pour over the dry ingredients. Cover thermos immediately and secure. Yield: 2 cups.

Creamy Country Soup

* 2 cups of instant nonfat dried milk powder

* 10 TBL tablespoon of cornstarch

* 1/4 Cup chicken bouillon granules

* 2 TBL tablespoons dried vegetable flakes

* 1 Tsp onion powder

1/2 teaspoon dried Marjoram

* 1/4 Tsp garlic powder

* 1/8 Tsp. white pepper

* 2 Cups of boiling hot water

Mix all ingredients together in a food processor/blender. Cover and process until vegetables are finely chopped. You can keep the mixture in an airtight container up to one year. Mix ingredients in boiling water until ready to use. Allow to simmer for between 20-30 minutes.

Yields: 16 servings

Cream of Potato soup

* 3/4 Cups instant mashed potatoes flakes

1 1/2 cups of dry milk powder

* 2 TBL spoons of chicken broth granules

* 2 Tbsp of minced onion dried

* 1 Tbsp dried Parsley

* 1/4 Tsp ground white pepper

* 1/4 Tsp dried Thyme

* 1 1/2 tsp seasoning salt

* 2 cups of boiling water

Combine ingredients in boiling water and simmer until soup is made.

Yields 6 servings

Soup for Chicken and Rice

* 2 cups of uncooked long grains brown rice

* 1/2 cup of chicken bouillon, granules

* 4 Tsp dried gargano

* 1 Tsp. white pepper

* 3 cups of water

* 1 TBL teaspoon butter or margarine

To make soup, heat the butter and water in a saucepan. Add 2/3 cup of soup mix. Reduce heat, cover, and simmer the mixture for 30-35 mins or until rice is tender.

Yields 6 servings

Hearty Bean Soup

* 2 cups of dried yellow split Peas

* 2 Cups green dried splitpeas

* 2 cups of dried lima Beans

* 2 Cups dried pinto bean

* 2 Cups of great northern bean dried

* 1 Cup minced dried minced onions

1 Cup dried carrots

1 Cup dried celery

* 12 sun-dried tomatoes, chopped

* 1 1/2 Tsp dried cumin

* 1 Tbsp dried marjoram Leaves

* 1 1/2 Tsp garlic powder

* 1 Tbsp onion salt

* 1/4 teaspoon pepper

* 8 Cups water

* One ham bone (for flavouring) - *This ingredient shouldn't be stored with other ingredients. It should only be used in cooking.

In a large saucepan, combine the soup mix with water. Bring to boil the soup mix on high heat. Allow it to boil for 2 minutes. Turn down heat and simmer for two hours or until beans become tender. Removing meat from bones, add to soup.

Creamy Cheese Soup

* 1 Cup of powdered Cheese

* 3 tablespoons of chicken bouillon, granules

* 1/2 Tsp. pepper

* 1 Cup of vegetable broth mix

* 3 TBL spoon of dried Parsley Flakes

* 3 Cups of nonfat, dry milk or coffee creamer

* 5 TBL spoons cornstarch

* 8 Cups of boiling hot water

Mix all ingredients in a bowl with some boiling water. Let soup cool for 5-10 minutes.

Yields: 8 servings

Dishwashing Liquid - Rubbish Bags - Disposable Plates - Cups, Cups & Cutlery

There will be times when things you rely on such as water are not as easy to find as they were in the past. This is a problem that can affect any survival situation. It won't be easy to turn on water taps and get endless amounts of clean, healthy water. Instead, you will need to work for it.

Keep your kitchen clean to prevent any potential diseases.

Dishwashing Solution

This is one item that will not break the bank, and it doesn't take much space. It's a great deal if you can find it at a discount and the stronger, more concentrated versions are available. This will allow you to get more bang for the buck, as water will be scarce and you won't have to wash your hands every five minutes.

Paper plates, cups, utensils

You should limit your washing if you don't have a water source. The excessive amount of water used can be more beneficial for you to stay hydrated.

The easiest solution is to not wash anything or do the minimum. If you use plastic accessories or paper, you can just toss them away.

Rubbish Bags

You're bound to have rubbish. It must not be left unattended in your safe house, home or bunker. A supply of strong, durable rubbish bags is necessary that they won't break or tear.

You don't want them running around the yard and burning rubbish close to you. This could lead to unwanted attention. Plan to complete at least one rubbish sweep per week and take as little rubbish as you can.

Once you have it taken, spend as much time disguise the tracks and rubbish to and from your property. Do not do your rubbish runs the same day each week. Instead, do them on different days.

Chapter 7: Medical Supplies

There are only so many things you can keep and prepare for. The hard part is choosing what is important to you and what will be most beneficial. While having all the necessary surgery is hard, knowing how to treat someone with a heart disease is even harder.

You must stock the most commonly used items. Items that treat burns and other illnesses will be the most important.

We'll be discussing the best medical equipment to have on hand in the next chapter.

Alcohol

There are many ways to use alcohol. You can drink it, trade it, or use it for medical purposes. Any serious preppers cellar will have a lot to offer. But, what type of alcohol should they be stockpiling?

Even if alcohol is not something you drink, it's still a good idea to keep a large inventory of alcohol. If you don't drink it it will last even longer.

As a disinfectant, you can put alcohol on wounds to keep them from getting infected. You can also use it to numb areas for your dental work. A quick way to kill someone is to use alcohol. It will be much easier for someone in crisis to get alcohol than it is to access modern medical supplies.

How much alcohol should you have in your stockpile?

If you don't drink alcohol, vodka, whiskey, and even rum are the most cost-effective and easiest to keep in stock. When you're choosing which types or brands of alcohol to purchase, price will be a major consideration. However buying the best brands won't necessarily affect how they perform in an emergency situation.

These are the top two things you need to be looking for.

* Any alcohol that has an alcohol percentage of more than 60% may be used as a surgical alcohol

* Alcohol with a higher than 40% alcohol percentage can be used for disinfecting wounds

If the bottles do not have proof, the easiest way to find your alcohol percent is to divide it in half.

The shelf life is the next thing to consider when stockpiling alcohol.

You shouldn't drink beer or cool drinks. Their shelf lives are too short. Most cases last between one and two year.

Stocking liquors can be tricky as they are often high in sugar and alcohol.

Wine is not ideal for stockpiling. Also, it can't even be used medicinally like spirits. Some wine may last longer and even improve if kept in a dry, cool place. But most wines won't.

Everclear is the best choice for a value-for-money spirit to have in your stockpile. The high alcohol content makes it almost unpalatable, but you're unlikely to enjoy it.

There will be many kinds of alcohol that can be stored, but they will all perform the same task. If you are only interested in spirits, you could store whiskey, brandy, rum or gin along with vodka, vodka, Tequila, and Gin. The price of alcohol doesn't decrease a lot but you can get great value bottles for whiskey or vodka. You should keep them cool and dry. Keep them in crates, if possible, to avoid bottles being crushed or knocked over.

Bleach for Prepping

Most people have a bleach bottle in their laundry basket or under their kitchen sink. It is used to remove stains and whiten clothes. Bleach has many more uses. Bleach is useful in many situations.

There will be plenty of bleach for the task. The bleach is cheap to purchase so make sure you have enough. It is crucial that bleach not be stored in places where it could react with other chemicals or exposed to high heat.

In the next section we'll discuss bleach's uses in any disaster or survival situation.

One. Making your water safe

According to the CDC approximately eight drops, or 1/8th of a teaspoon, of bleach are enough to disinfect a gallon water. It is two drops per one liter if you use liter bottles. Once you have added the bleach, make sure it is well mixed and let the water sit for at the least 30-45 minutes before drinking. Additional drops may be required if the water appears very cloudy, or is extremely cold.

Two. Two.

One teaspoon of bleach should be used to one gallon water to clean the surfaces of food preparations. This will ensure that bacteria from raw meats does not cross-contaminate other food products. The same process can be used for plastic containers containing raw meats and other food items. But, give them at most 15-30 minutes to soak.

Three. Cleanse Fruits and Vegetables

Floods can lead water contamination, and fresh produce and vegetables may become contaminated by the water. Make a mixture of one teaspoon of bleach and one gallon water. Once the bleach has dissolved, rinse the vegetables and fruits. Let them soak for several days. Don't cut off the skin. This can cause contamination to the inside of the item.

Four. Get Rid Of Mold and Mildew

Mold can be dangerous and more deadly than people realize. Any mildew or mold buildup within your compound, home, or bunker can cause sickness or death. One cup bleach per gallon of water is sufficient to kill mildew. After mixing the mixture, allow it to rest for around 10-15 minutes. Finally, scrub any affected areas with a clean cloth. Make sure to have adequate airflow and that you wear the proper safety gear.

Five. Preventing the Spread of Illnesses & Diseases

To disinfect or clean the bedding and clothing of someone who is sick, you will need to do so immediately. To wash your bedding or clothes, use an approximate 1:100 ratio.

It is important not to mix bleach and other cleaning products. You could get poisonous gas if bleach is mixed with ammonia or other cleaning products. Wear appropriate safety equipment.

Soap

While you may not consider this to be essential, a large supply of soap is vital in the event of a disaster. This could include bars of soap or liquid soap as well as shampoo and conditioner. People around you will also be more susceptible to getting sick if they lose their ability to create basic sanitation. You can trade soap if it is kept in a dry, cool place.

First Aid Kit

It doesn't matter how important we think something should be in your first-aid kit. Someone will always argue that it is more important or less important.

Pre-made kits are the best choice for beginners. They will have everything you need for your short-term needs. If you want to prepare for a long-term situation, you can build your own kit. Everything depends on how much cash you have and how much time you are willing spend.

There are some items you will not need, which is why you shouldn't buy first aid kits already made. A second problem is that you can build your own first-aid kit. You'll be familiar with it, and you'll know exactly what it contains and where it is located.

We got this list from Red Cross to give you a good idea of what should be in an emergency kit and a first-aid kit.

First Aid Kit

Make sure you have a first aid kit at all times. Keep it handy in your cottage, car or boat. You should keep it dry and change out any worn or obsolete contents as often as possible.

This should be included in your first aid kit

* You can reach your emergency number for EMS/9-1-1 or your local poison control centre, as well as your personal doctor.

* Numbers for home and office phones to help family, friends, neighbors, and others who may be able to assist

* Sterile gauze pads or dressings in small and big squares for use over wounds

* Adhesive tape

* For holding dressings or making an arm wrap, use triangular and roll bandages.

* Adhesive bandages of various sizes

* Scissors

* Tweezers

* Safety pins

* Instant ice packs

* Disposable latex gloves (e.g. surgical or examination gloves)

* Flashlights with extra batteries, in a separate bag

* Antiseptic soaps and wipes

* Pencil & pad

* Emergency blanket

* Eye patches

* Thermometer

* Barrier devices like a pocket or face mask

* Coins are required for paying phones

* Canadian Red Cross first-aid manual

Emergency Supplies Kit

You should always have emergency supplies. Keep them in a backpack and a dufflebag so that they are easily accessible in case you need to evacuate.

* 4 Liters of water per person, per day (use sealed and unbreakable containers; replace the supply every six month).

* Pre-packaged or canned food that will not go bad and a can opener.

* A change of clothes, rain gear, walking shoes

* Pillows and sleeping bags

* A first aid kit (and prescription medications) that aren't expired.

* Toilet paper, and other personal supplies

* An additional pair of glasses

* A battery powered radio and flashlight.

* Don't spend too much cash

* An additional set of keys for your car

* A listing of your family physicians

* Important family information like a list if any medical conditions are present or medical devices used, such pacemakers.

* Photos of all your important identification (including health card numbers) for yourself and your family.

* Special items to be used by elderly and disabled household members

* Information about your family's cell phone and contacts

Kit for Emergency Car Kit

You should always keep an emergency kit in the car.

* A flashlight and radio with battery power, including extra batteries

* A blanket

* Booster (jumper) cables

* A fire extinguisher

* Canadian Red Cross manual and first aid kit

* Water bottles and high-energy foods that don't go bad.

* Maps of area

* A shovel

* Flares

* A kit for repairing and replacing tires

* Matches or a "survival" candle that can burn for many hours in a deep-can.

If you are interested in buying prepper-style emergency situations first aid kits, we also have some links to kits available online through Amazon.

First Aid Kit for Travel, Hiking, Camping, Travel, Cars and Bug Out Bags. 105 pieces. It costs $24.99 and is available HERE.

Stealth Tactical Bugout bag-2 Person, 72-hour Emergency Survival Kit. Brand Emergency Zone. You can order it HERE at a price of $249.99

We could keep listing survival bags and other medical bags. However, it is worth shopping around and reading reviews before you purchase an item.

Painkillers

It is not impossible to get hurt and have headaches. However, it will never go away. A good supply of painkillers will help you stay healthy. Almost! The truth is that painkillers can be very helpful, regardless of how severe the situation.

It's a good idea that you have enough painkillers to last you a long time. They have a long expiry time and, if needed, they will only get weaker.

There are many painkillers that you can choose from. They all have different uses. Make sure they are kept dry and in their original packaging. Don't worry if you have many, they will be extremely useful for bartering in any SHTF scenario.

Sanitation and Toilet Paper

If you're planning to spend any time in a bunker, compound, or other type of bugout location, you need to ensure that sanitation plans are in place. It is likely that you have already taken care of the sanitation situation if your location has been constructed. If you're planning to live in your house, then you will need a solution to your sanitation problem.

You'd be annoyed if you went a few days without using the toilet. If there are more than one person living nearby, you'll be searching for an alternative very quickly.

Setting up a small sanitation station is the easiest way to temporarily solve sanitation problems. It doesn't have the cost or complexity of an expensive and complicated sanitation station. A basic sanitation station is a simple setup that includes a sanitation bucket, toilet paper, baby diapers, and a treatment for sewage. You can also use composting toilets and septic tanks to create more advanced systems.

There are many different types of toilets on the market, and each one is good for a certain amount of time. Consider the time frame you have to plan and buy the toilet system that will best suit your needs.

You can clean your butt with whatever you want, but you'll regret it after a few weeks or days. This may seem obvious but it is important to keep a good supply of toilet paper handy.

You can use this information to calculate how much toilet tissue you need. It is best to keep it dry. Toilet paper takes up much space so don't store too much. You can also buy double-length rolls, which are generally rolled closer. It doesn't have to be fancy.

Chapter 8: Survival Items

Matches, Lighters, and Flints

To light a gas fire, to heat the house, to keep it warm, or to burn your rubbish, you will need a means of doing this. They won't take much up in your prepping area and won't cost much. You can stockpile matches, lighter fluid, spare lighter flints, and even a Zippo.

When you need to create a fire in any other way, you'll wish you had more lighters! You should keep your lighters dry and keep them away form other flammable substances like alcohol or chemicals.

Bottled Water. Walter Filters. Water Tablets. Water Purifiers.

People can live long lives without food. In fact, it is possible for humans to go several weeks without food. Water is the killer. Water is what sustains us all.

Water is an essential part of any survival situation. Water must be used for cooking, cleaning, bathing, and other purposes.

Every water plan should include several options, such as how to store bottled water, clean, filter and purify water, or look for water sources. In most cases, dedicated preppers with safe locations will dig their own wells so they don't have any dependence on others. However, if the water is damaged by an earthquake or flood, it might need to be treated until it stabilizes.

Preppers have to have plenty of water and places where they can refill it as they need. The main problem is that water storage takes up too much space.

Another solution is to set your home up to capture rainwater. If this happens, you can place a water tank somewhere on your property. Rainwater will then be used to replenish the tank.

Bottled water will be your best option for drinking clean water. Large gallon jugs are available. Keep them in a cool, dry place. You can expect it to last a very long time. However, it is important to regularly rotate through your bottled waters to ensure it doesn't sit in one place for too long. Commercially available water has already been treated and approved by government.

Here are some quick tips to store your bottled Water:

* Keep it dark and cool.

* Place it on concrete only

* Avoid stacking stacks too high. They could crush bottom bottles and cause stacks to collapse on you.

* Make sure to rotate your bottled water supply in order to keep it fresh

* Never leave empty water bottles around. You should use it or throw it away after 3-4 Days.

You're going to need more water than you realize. So, make sure you have as much water as you can. It's safer to store water than go out looking for it.

At least 20-30gallons of water should be allowed per person. Minimum storage requirements are at least 3 months' worth, or 90gallons. This could be stored in large drums. Or, if you have the space, place a rainwater collection tank on a patio.

Every serious prepper should learn how to purify their water and make them safe to drink.

Boiling water makes it safe to drink. It is one of oldest and most straightforward ways to do this. It is best to boil the water for no less than ten minutes before you can drink it. The main problem is that boiling water won't make water taste or look good.

Water can be filtered using rocks, charcoal, and sand. This will improve the water's appearance and flavor, but it won't remove all bacteria and contaminants. The recommendation is to filter the water and boil it.

If you are in a hurry, you can use iodine to clean your water. But it is not recommended due to other reasons. Iodine is poisonous and can cause you to become sick. Iodine treatment takes around 30 minutes if the water temperature is high. For every gallon you will need about ten drops.

Another way to treat water is by using chlorine. The tablets are ready to be used.

One way to treat water is with chlorine bleach. You only need one teaspoon per gallon of 10 drops.

* Do not use pool chlorine. It is much stronger

* Do not use scented bleaches

* Make sure it hasn't expired

There are many options for commercial water treatment systems.

All Kinds of Batteries, Solar Battery Chargers, Battery Chargers

Batteries are essential for all devices, including flashlights, radios, GPS units, and flashlights. In any emergency situation, the electricity is often the first thing that goes. If you have a lot of property, it is likely that you have a generator. It shouldn't be a problem. But, if there's no safe place to store your generator and you just want to have a bag for emergencies, you may need another alternative.

There are a variety of options available. You have the option of solar or rechargeable batteries. There are many options available, and each model is different in terms of size, power, cost, and price.

Another option is the USB Solar Charger. It acts as a battery bank. You can plug your device in via a USB cable. These charge well and don't lose power if it is cloudy or overcast.

You should remember to buy all your electronics and chargers, and make them uniform. You don't want to need different chargers and cables for every device. The entire bag is extremely lightweight and fits easily into your bug-out bag.

You might be able to buy larger solar panel if your space is larger, like a home or house.

Be aware that light can have a double-edged edge. If you intend to have lights on and other devices running, then you must ensure that you have sufficient lighting security. It is a great way to show someone that you are in the area with a lot of solar panel arrays.

Sleeping Bags. Swags. Tents. Tarps.

You do not need shelters or tents if there is a pre-planned location where you can bug out. However, if your plan is to move around until you find somewhere you like, then you will need shelters such as a tent and/or swag.

You should balance your shelter need with your weight. You shouldn't be carrying 200 lbs. Not only will it be difficult to move 200 lbs., but it could also make you a target for desperate individuals. To maintain your speed and maneuverability, balance your B.O.B.

You should not advertise that you have a wonderful tent if you intend to bring it along. Your tent can be camouflaged with branches or an old cover to make it invisible.

If it's just you, you'll only need one-person tent. This will keep you protected and safe from the elements. You will need a good quality tent, sleeping bag, and tarps. For camouflage purposes or to make a screen, place one tarp underneath your tent and another over it.

Better sleeping bags will be lighter, and they are better for colder climates. You will be able to roll them up and make a smaller bag, which allows you to store other essentials. A good tent and sleeping bag can be a valuable addition to any

B.O.B. They are also an excellent investment.

Torches, candles, lanterns and lanterns

It is quite obvious that in any situation of disaster where power goes out, you will need to have alternative light sources.

* Candles

* Lanterns

* Torches

* Lamps

It is important to understand that, without power and waiting for it to return, you will have no choice but to live from sunrise to sunset. While you could stock candles and lanterns as well as run a generator to supply power, what will the resources cost? If you don't have to, it is best to just operate during daylight hours.

It is a good idea to have large emergency candles on hand. These candles will last a long time and give you the best value. You can also use them as headlights, lanterns, or battery powered torches. You will be able to use your headlights or headlamps in dark conditions while still being able to use your hands. These can be recharged during the day using solar battery chargers. Then they can be used at night.

You want to make sure that your fuel supplies are preserved if you have large compounds or bunkers with access. This will reduce generator noise.

Sound, sound, and light can travel long distances and attract lots of unwanted visitors. If you will be using the night light, you should confine it to specific areas. To keep others from seeing your location and what you are doing, you should cover windows and doors.

Rope

It's a shame that you don't have enough rope for your B.O.B. Rope is an essential item for preppers. It is lightweight, portable, light, cost-effective, versatile, and easy to use.

So which type of rope should I use?

Avoid "laid rope" and twisted rope. This isn't a very good choice and can quickly rot. They can sink and are very strong but they will only last so long as you take good care of them.

Climbing rope can be extremely durable, but it is also very heavy. You will have to carry it around with you, decreasing the number of other items.

Thin Guy Lines may be good for some things, but not for others.

Rubber cords and bungee cords work well for attaching loads. They are lightweight, so be sure to include a few in your kit.

Paracord is a popular type of rope that preppers will use. Paracord is strong, lightweight, and affordable. Paracord can be used in a variety of lengths. It can be purchased online at Amazon.

Paracord: What are you using it for?

* Fishing

* Building traps, snares

* Boot laces

* Flossing

* Climbing and hiking

* Sewing thread

* Building a shelter

* Tying down your tent or canvas tarp

* Keeping your gear in one place

* Make sure your items are secured on top of your car/motorcycle

* Repairing any damaged or torn equipment

* Making a tourniquet

* Attaching things in your backpack

* Trip wires

* Rigging a pulley to lift heavy gears or other items

* Building ladders

* Making a hammock for sleep

* Building a raft

* Making a catapult/sling and many more! !

Chapter 9: Hunting, Gathering and Self Defense

Defense Weapons, Guns. Rifles. Shotguns. Pistols. Crossbows.

It is not difficult for law and order in any crisis to collapse. Your first problem will be desperate people who aren't prepared for any kind of disaster. Once the chaos has subsided, you will need to deal with those who would rather have others provide for them than take care of themselves.

I don't recommend any weapons. Much depends on how someone has used weapons in the past and what their personal preferences are. This is a brief overview with some tips.

If you're planning to set up a compound, bunker or home, then you need to plan how to defend yourself. The best way to avoid being noticed is to convince people that you aren't worth it.

It all depends on how much storage space you have, and what laws you have in your state or country. Before you begin to stockpile weapons, check your laws. !

It is strongly recommended that you attend the right training courses to ensure that you are fully trained if you intend to purchase guns for hunting or self-defense.

Your best weapon is you. Develop a plan of defense. Make sure everyone knows their roles.

1. Shotguns are a good choice as a self-defense weapon. You have many options for different models, and you can also choose different shells. It looks great from close up, but it may be difficult for you to swing around in the interior when you are close enough.

2. For self-defense within the home, a pistol or any other handgun is a great choice. It's easier to use than a shotgun,

and you can get it closer. You can't use it as easily as a shotgun. It takes a lot of practice to master the gun.

3. While it's not as practical in your home, it does have its advantages. For example, a bow and crossbow is a great weapon. It can be used to defend or hunt, but it is slower to reload and therefore quieter.

4. A good way to stop most people entering your home is pepper spray or mace. However, they must be within close proximity to you so that you can avoid spraying yourself.

5. When you are being attacked, collapsible talons can be very useful for self defense. These can be used if your attacker does not have a weapon. However, you will need to engage in a fight with them.

6. Diverse bladed weapons such as machetes. Other miscellaneous tools such

as picks, picks, and hammers can also be used. While these are better than being killed, they require you to get close and personal when you are attacked.

It is crucial to ensure the safety of those around you, especially young children.

Ammunition, Arrows, & Arrow Heads

It doesn't matter if you have weapons. If you run out, they won't be of much use. Be sure to have enough ammunition for any weapon you plan to purchase.

If you plan on using bows, it is important to keep a stock of shafts or arrowheads.

The same goes for shotguns, rifles, or pistols. Stock ammunition that will last a lifetime and any spare parts that may be needed. You can also stock up on the equipment that you will need for making your own ammunition.

Stock up on enough food to last you for a specified period. Double it later!

Fishing Equipment, Collapsible Rods. Hooks and Line.

One item keeps cropping up in discussions on bug out bags is the survival fishing tin. A majority of survival fishing tins have a few fishing items along with other useful items.

These are the essentials for any survival fishing boat:

* At least 50 ft of sturdy monofilament fish line. This line must weigh 20 lb or more. It's not meant for sports fishing. To prevent your line from getting tangled up and catching, you can wrap it around any stick.

* A variety of hooks to suit different fish species.

* Bobbers/floats. In an emergency, any type of material will float.

* Sinkers or weights of a variety different sizes.

* Use fishing lures or soft-plastics to fish in the best area.

You can buy pre-made or purchased emergency fishing tins. If you have some fishing knowledge, then we recommend building your own. This will ensure you get the right gear for you. Another great idea is to visit your local fishing store to get their recommendations.

Similar to hunting equipment, fishing gear won't guarantee your success in catching fish. Once you've decided to use the items in a set, go out and find some waterways nearby.

You can't carry your fishing rod everywhere if you are just going out and about. You'll already be carrying a lot of gear if your bow or rifle is with you. You will have more space for fishing rods if your bunker compound is bugging in.

Online you will find many options for collapsible and Telescopic fishing rods. This might be something worth looking into if your space is available and you can lift your weight.

Survival Gardening Seeds

It is not difficult, but it can be hard to grow vegetables and fruits from scratch if you have never tried. You cannot just throw seeds into the ground and expect fresh fruit and vegetables all your lives.

But that doesn't mean you can't stockpile seeds for when the worst happens. If you're planning on being on the go in any type of disaster, you won't have much need to plant a vegetable garden.

You will want to pay attention to these aspects during any survival situation.

* The calories you will require

* The protein you'll need

* The required fat content

* How to store winter croppings

* The food that you need to feed the people you have

* How much room you have to grow what your need

* How long it will take to grow the items you require.

* How to keep seeds safe for future crops

* What kind of fruits or plants are you allowed to grow in your locality?

* How you can preserve what you grow

* What tools do you need for growing your crops?

* How to prevent pests from eating your crops

For a survival gardening program to be successful, you must address each of these issues. If you do not plan on leaving your home, you have the chance to set up your survival garden immediately.

Even though you can't survive solely on plants, a decent garden is a great addition to any other food stocks. You can also supplement your MREs and preserved meats with fresh fruit or vegetables.

You don't need to maintain a diet-friendly, slim meal plan in any survival situation. You're not trying to lose weight but gain weight. Your body should allow you to skip a meal, if necessary.

The following are the top crops you can grow and store in any survival situation:

* Potatoes- These potatoes are high in protein, and they can be stored in dark, cool places far from other fruits.

* Winter squash is high in vitamins and starch and can be dried for extended storage.

* Corn – Sweet corn is great fresh but does not store well. The other varieties of corn can be stored well if dried properly.

* Beans are great fresh and they can be stored well.

* Sunflower Seeds are excellent when dried and stored. High in protein and fat.

You can purchase specific seeds that are prepackaged for preppers. They usually last between 5 and 20 year.

This is a very basic guide to survival gardening. You could easily write a whole book about it. Don't wait until the last moment to learn how gardening is done. While it can take many years, starting now will help you to grow your garden.

Survival Axe

There are literally hundreds upon thousands of survival axes. We aren't going to give you a comprehensive list of all the various axes, or what each one is good for. We're only going to discuss some of the reasons you need one.

Every tool is useful in any survival situation. However, you only have so much gear to pack in your bug out bag. While you might have the option to store tools in a bunker, bug out location or compound, you may not have enough space. A survival axe is a useful tool for those who are always on the move.

For the following reasons, you can use your survival axe:

* Self-defense

* Building a shelter

* Hacking firewood

* As a hammer

* Build a shelter

* Breaking into properties

* Protecting your building

Skilled Survival is a great resource for information on survival axes.

Compass and Maps

If you are thinking of bugging out or in, a map is an essential tool. A complete set includes maps for your region, state, and country. You will also require a high-quality compasse and the skills necessary to use it.

Don't wait for the SHTF - take a course to learn how you can read a map or compass. Then, practice your bug out plans with your map and bug bag. Then plan your route and track yourself. Push yourself to the limits.

Survivopedia provides a detailed article on maps and compasses and how they can be used.

YouTube offers many video options.

Chapter 10: Miscellaneous Items

This chapter will cover all of the items that we could not fit into one section. There are going to be items that are more valuable than others. In the end, it comes down largely to how much you can bring with you. If you have a good location for storing equipment, you will be able store more. However, if your only option is to carry everything with you, and you're not able to move around, then each item should serve a purpose.

Scissors

How often do your household members look for a pair or scissors? You use them all the time. It doesn't matter if you have an emergency. One pair of good scissors can save you a lot. You can use the same scissors as a knife to make a substitute, or you can purchase lightweight camping scissors.

Duct Tape

You can use a few rolls to help in any emergency situation. It can be used for repairs to tarps, tents, or wrapping equipment. You will need at least one roll.

Screws and Nails for Building Supplies

A few packets of screws or nails are a great way to secure your home or make it safe for the night. Although you cannot carry an entire hardware shop with you while on foot, you can still carry a small assortment of screw and nail items.

It is important to have a number of nails and screws on hand in case you need them. Sheets of plywood work well for creating temporary walls and sealing up windows. It's a great idea to lay the plywood sheets upstairs, in an attic, or with some additional lumber.

There won't be any time to go to the local hardware shop. You'll need to make sure you have everything you need before disaster strikes.

Cigarettes and Tobacco

Even if they don't smoke cigarettes or tobacco, these items can still be traded for valuable other items. You can store them properly and they will last for several years. Keep them cool and keep away from any liquids that could contaminate.

Silver and Gold

A small inventory of gold and silver can make a big difference in the event of a natural disaster. Imagine that all the current coins and bank notes would cease to be useful. Bartering with others could be made possible by pure gold and sterling coins.

How to Books (Hard Copies).

While you might not be able do everything before the worst happens, you can have manuals or how-to books to help you learn. If you're not sure that your Kindle will always have power, you shouldn't store them all. A good book can be read over and over again.

Find bargain books for sale that may come in useful one-day and get them cheaply. They won't fit in your bag, but you can keep them safe and organized. They should be wrapped in plastic, or stored somewhere where they can't be damaged by the weather.

Camouflage clothing and boots

For hunting and low-key activities, you'll need good outdoor clothes. Camouflage clothes to hunt, and scout, sturdy walking shoes, spare shoe laces, and any other clothing you can think of. A good waterproof jacket, or even spats. If you plan to be out walking all day.

Chapter 11: Planning Short, Medium & Long Term

A survival pantry is where you store your food, water, or other essential supplies to survive. It is an enclosed, separate, protected, VENTILATED, and UPDATED pantry. There are many locations in your home you could use to store a survival stash. Ideally, your pantry should be near the place you plan to stay in an emergency.

When searching for the right space, you need to know four characteristics about every survival pantry.

*SEPARATE FROM your daily pantry or supplies. You don't want rely on your survival foods pantry for your daily food needs. You should leave your survival food pantry alone, except when it is getting near the end of its useful life or you are in dire need. People don't realize that having a healthy food supply is a great safety net for when you are in trouble. It is impossible to know when you might lose your job or when someone in your family will get sick, making it difficult to purchase food.

*EASILY UPDATE/ROTED is important. You don't want to pick a place that is hard to reach. You must be able and willing to rotate your stock, as well as inspect for any signs that may indicate spoilage. Canned food will last for years but can spoil at times. It's not something you want sitting in your survival foods pantry. It can make your home a dangerous place. If you want to add new items to your collection, it must be possible to place them behind or at the back of your existing items. If you can't do this in your pantry, you might be inclined to neglect your rotation duties.

*VENTILATION IS VERY important. Although basements and root cells make great pantry spaces, they must be properly ventilated. Temperature control is also important. Food labels that state food has an expiry date of 20 years or 5 year are indicative that the food was stored in a safe environment. It is important to ventilate in order to reduce mold growth. You don't want your food supply to be destroyed by toxic mold. Your storage area should:

* Ventilated

* No extreme heat -- above 80 degrees Fahrenheit

* No extreme cold -- below 50 degrees Fahrenheit

* No dampness

* Outside of direct sunlight

*PROTECTED from potential looters. You don't want your pantry to be publicized. There will be lots of people, probably some of your neighbors who didn't take the time and planned to store. Your supplies will be protected from those you consider to be friends. The majority of your food storage should be hidden. To hide your food, you can create a fake wall in a basement. You should also protect your pantry against pests like ants, mice, or roaches. It can be frustrating to find that all your hard earned money for food storage has been destroyed by an invading pest.

You should do your best to meet these requirements. You don't need to have an underground bunker to make sure you and your family are safe. These are the qualities you should strive for. However, as a prepper, you know that you only have what you can afford.

Planning for the Short, Medium and Long Term

Rome wasn't built in a day. Your survival food pantry is no different. It doesn't make any sense to borrow money to buy food. Your planning should be done in small bites. To do this, you will need to start with short, medium, and ultimately long-term planning.

The short term will be your first milestone. This will provide enough food and water to sustain your family for at least 30 days. You should expect to spend at least twice as long to make that much food.

Medium term should have 3 to 6 moist of food and water. If you don't have enough space to store your emergency pantry, it can become a problem. You might have to find a way to store your food and water in a small space.

Long-term would be considered a survival food storage that will last your family for at least one year. This will take some time and take up lots of space. This goal is one that many preppers strive to attain, but it requires dedication and time.

Plan Your Pantry-Food

These tips can help you plan what ingredients you should include in your pantry. Be prepared, you will need to do some math. It is important to remember that food storage is determined by calories and not quantity. Today we eat three meals per meal with some snacking. Unless your diet is very strict, you may not pay much attention how many calories you are consuming. It's about eating until you feel satisfied. You may not be allowed to eat 3 meals a day in a survival situation. It is possible that you will only be allowed to eat one meal and have to snack between. The right food can help you survive and thrive.

Let's get started with a very simple formula to help you plan your pantry.

Consider that every member of your family must consume at least 2000 calories each day in order to survive. While technically, children will require less, it is still a good idea for them to have some food on hand. A man can survive on only 2,000 calories per person, but they should have more if they are doing labor-intensive tasks, such as. An extra 500 to 1000 calories a day would be a great thing for men who hunt, split wood, or dig.

Let's say that you have a family consisting of 4.4 persons. This is 2000 calories x 8,000 calories per person.

You must ensure you have enough food for your family to meet their daily calorie requirements. Read labels. Preppers love canned and freeze-dried foods. They last for years without spoiling. Imagine that you plan to prep the bulk of your meals using freeze-dried foods. (This is a good option, if the price is right).

16 portions will be found in a #10 can. Don't let 16 servings fool you into believing that it will feed 4 meals. It won't. Look at the can's calorie information.

Here's another assumption. Let us assume that each meal of frozen meals you offer to the family contains 250 calories. This is pretty common for canned and freeze-dried foods.

Each family member requires 2000 calories per day. 2000 calories/250 calories per meal = 8 meals are required per person to achieve daily calorie intake.

Each can contains 16 servings. 16 servings per can are divided into 8 meals per head = 2. Each day, two people will require one can of food. You would need two cans of food for a family with four people.

60 cans frozen-dried food is required to meet your 30-day food supply.

Wowza! This formula will calculate how many meals you'd need to last 60 days, 90 days, or for whatever time period. You wouldn't want to feed the entire family the exact same meal every single day. However, this gives you an idea of what food you will need to start stocking your survival food pantry.

A survival situation is where nutrition is as crucial as any other day. You should try to prepare balanced meals. Consider a food chain and make sure you have a food supply that can provide your family with healthy, varied and nutritious meals. In another chapter, we'll talk about the foods you should keep to provide your family with nutritious meals.

Water - Planning Your Pantry

Water is the most difficult aspect in a survival food storage pantry. You need a lot of water! It is bulky and heavy. How much are you going to need?

Every family member requires 1 gallon of water every day.

If you did the math right, you will realize that this is 120 gallons water per month for a family consisting of four families. This is a lot. Unfortunately, 120gallons of water isn't enough to supply enough water for drinking or basic cleaning. It is not enough water for serious housecleaning or to take a shower.

Despite the difficulties associated with water storage, you must still do it. It's up to you to devise a solution to keep enough water to last your family. This chapter will provide some suggestions on how to achieve this. We must first remember another rule for survival.

All water can be considered unsafe for consumption.

The water can be considered safe to drink if it has been commercially packaged and kept in BPA-free bottles in good conditions. You should only drink the water as it is, and not purify it.

Water that hasn't had treatment is not safe for human health. It is risky even to attempt it. It is a good idea to have water purification techniques on hand for your emergency supplies. You can boil the water, if you have enough money. The most common way to purify your water is with household bleach. However, the shelf life for this product is only 6 months. You should watch the rotation of bleach if you intend to use it to purify your water. Iodine may also be an option. But remember that anyone allergic to shellfish can get iodine poisoning.

Filters may be an option, however they are not purifiers. They can't remove viruses. You can choose to purify water first and then filter it to make it better and clearer.

Consider this question as you build your survival food storage: Are you going to be bugging in, or bugging out? Don't waste time in building a food pantry for your future move. It will likely be impossible and difficult to haul all your food, water and other items from Point A to Point B. Even if your plan is to bug out, it will be necessary to keep at most 3 days of food and water. To be safe, you should have a minimum of three days worth of food and water to last you until you are able to evacuate.

Chapter 12: How to Store Water More Effectively

Let's look at water storage. It's a challenging task but it is possible. Your location and plans for where you will store water are important factors. Ideally, rural living should be the goal. To truly thrive in a situation where the country or the entire world is being affected by a devastating event, you will need land and plenty of space.

You should assume that the power grid won't be available. If there is no power, it means that public water systems will go out of business. They will not purify the water, making it unsafe for drinking.

Private Wells

You will need a handpump to pump water from your own well. The electric well pump you have will not work. If you are willing and able to invest, solar pumps are available. You should not assume that water coming from your well is safe. You will never know what could have happened downstream. It is possible for water to be contaminated by dead animals, or it could be the result of a chemical leakage. Always clean the water before using it.

Cisterns

These vessels look great if you have enough space. You can either place these huge vessels high up on a hill, or you can bury them in the ground. This is a great way to conceal your water supply. Cisterns can come in different sizes. There are 500-gallon containers up to 1000 gallons. If the cistern has been buried, you will require a hand pump to remove the water. If it is on a hill you can benefit from gravity.

Bottled Water

Bottled water is quick and easy but can take up too much space and be quite expensive. For those times when you are unable to get water purified, it would be a smart idea to have some bottled water available. You may think, "Hey! I will just buy milk jugs to bottle my own water." But you don't want old milk containers. They will soon be ruined and leak everywhere. Old soda bottles, 2-liter soda and juice bottles can be used. The bottles can be washed with soap and water, then refilled with tap water. Some people add a small amount of bleach to their tap water to preserve it. Most tap water is already treated using chlorine. It is not necessary to add additional bleach. You should change the water in your home-bottled water about every 6 months. Refill the water with the water you use to water your garden.

Rain Barrels

This is a great alternative and it's almost free. You can make your rain barrel yourself for $10 or buy one at Home Depot. As much rainwater as possible from your roof should be poured into as many barrels and containers as possible. Rainwater is safe to consume. However, since it comes in contact with your roof, gutters and other structures, it can become contaminated.

Backyard Ponds

You can actually drink pond water provided that it is purified. It takes very little to create a pond. You can choose to have a small pond lined with plastic or a larger pond with an au natural floor, which means it has a sandy, dirt floor. Fish can be added to the pond to make it a food source. If your pond water is cloudy, you can fill your vessel only with the water between the dirt on its bottom and the green layer. This will help filter your pond's water before it is purified.

Swimming Pools/Hot Tubs

If you have either one of these items, you will always have plenty of water. After the power goes off, it is best to wait three days before you purify the water. This allows the chlorine to air out and reduce its concentration to safe levels. Rain will replenish the water.

Chapter 13: How to Store Food More Efficiently

Storing food can be so crucial. You should maximize space and get as much shelf-life out of your food as possible. You must plan to live without power. This means you won't have refrigeration. You won't find a way to get steaks out of the freezer. This means that you will have to choose between fresh meat and canned, frozen, or dehydrated meat. It's time to discuss the storage of all the food you plan on stocking up for your survival foods pantry.

Shelving

Once you have a good idea of the food you need to stock up, you need to decide how you will store it. The rule of thumb is to keep food at 6 inches above the surface. In the event of MINOR flooding, this will keep your food dry and safe. Although 6 inches may not seem like much, it will ensure that your food is safe and dry in the event of flooding.

Make sure shelves have lipping on the top to prevent food sliding forward. This is especially important if your home is near railway tracks, earthquakes, or other vibrations that can cause food to slide forward. You don't want to be hit by a can of chili while you're riding high with your food pantry. If the shelf isn't shaped like a lip, you have plenty of options. It works!

To keep your food safe, you could also tie rope about 3 inches from the shelving. Also, you could use a piece wood as a front. It's all about being creative in order to ensure your food is safe.

Food-Grade Buckets

Food-grade 5-gallon plastic buckets are the best friend for preppers. They are indispensable. They are your best option for keeping food fresh and protected from pests. They are easy to stack and can prevent food spillage if shelves move or fall. Restaurants and bakeries can tell you if they will allow you to either buy or take their old buckets. These items are often given away by restaurants. One man's trash is almost always another man's treasure. You will need to cover the buckets with lids. They don't need lids. Avoid using buckets that may have contained chemicals or fertilisers.

Mylar bags

These bad boys are a favorite of preppers. They don't keep mice out, contrary to popular belief. They will however repel pests such ants as cockroaches. Your dried grains and beans should be placed in the Mylar bags, sealed and placed in a 5-gallon bucket. Some items can be kept in this manner for up to 20 year. Do yourself a favor by purchasing bags in bulk. They'll be useful. Even pasta can be stored in bags, and placed on your shelf. Be sure to label everything. There are many options available for sealing the bag. Most bags can either be heat sealed using an iron, or a Foodsaver-type tool. The bags protect food from oxygen, light and moisture. These three factors can cause food loss and shorten shelf life.

Kitchen Necessities

You'll need to learn to cook with minimal fuss. Now, take a look in your own kitchen. How do I open a can of canned food or make chili? There are likely to be an electric can opener, microwave, or coffee maker that will make your life simpler. It's the time to get back to "the Dark Ages"!

Here is a list you'll want to keep in your survival foods pantry.

* Manual can opener

* Manual grain mill

* You can make or buy a solar stove

* Percolated coffee maker

* Hand mixer

* Dutch oven

Cast iron cookware is ideal for cooking over an open fireplace

* Sterno stove

* Coleman stove - Store plenty of fuel/propane tanks

* Hand-cranked food strainer

* Heavy-duty hotpads

* Hand-cranked blender

What to store

This is what you've been waiting to see, right? What should you store in your survival stash? Are you ready for another survival tip?

Only keep what your eat today.

Do not waste your time or money on buying frozen or canned carrots for your family if they don't like them. Because the world went to hell in a handbasket, your taste buds won't change. Even though you might eat the carrots if your stomach was empty, you are building a survival food pantry to ensure you won't be starving. The stress of convincing your kids to eat the carrots is unnecessary. You can give your children what they want today, and you will have a much simpler life. Picky eaters are a problem.

We'll break this down into food types. Make sure you choose what you and the family eat and that you stockpile it. Diversifying your meal options is vital. There is something called food fatigue. If you eat canned chilli every day for a month, then your body will rebel. You may experience severe intestinal upset and even dehydration. Keep your body happy by changing things up. This list contains standard grocery items as well as frozen-dried, canned, dried and canned products.

Grains

* Wheat

* Flour

* Cornmeal

* Oats

* Rice

Legumes/Beans

* Pinto beans

* Navy beans

* Kidney beans

* Black beans are excellent for making patties in burgers

Fruit

* Canned fruits -- whatever your family loves

* Great snacks with dehydrated fruits

* Freeze dried fruits -- either eat them plain or add some flavor to give it a more "normal" taste

Vegetables

* Canned veggies -- any variety you prefer; opt for low-sodium varieties if possible

* Dehydrated vegetables

* To make a hearty stew from frozen vegetables, toss them in with rice

Protein/Meat

* Tuna

* Salmon

* Spam

* Chicken

* Peanut butter -- high in protein

* Jerky

Dairy

* Powdered Butter

* Powdered eggs

* Instant milk -- best for drinking

* Powdered milk -- best used for cooking

* Powdered cheese

Spices

* Salt

* Pepper

* Garlic salt & powder

* Bay leaves

* All-seasoning

Baking

* Baking soda

* Baking powder

* Cooking oils

* Shortening

*Yeast -- This can lead to a short shelf-life.

Grocery Store Articles

* Pasta

* Crackers

* Granola

* Candy

* Chocolate

* Sugar

* Honey

* Coffee

* Tea

* Nuts

* Chocolate bars

* Chili, ravioli, Spaghettios, etc...

* Canned beans

* Tomato sauce

* Macaroni Cheese

* Don't add sugar to drink mixes

This list does not include everything. The best thing to do is to go through your pantry. What food do they have? This is what you need to buy. Because you'll be making all your meals from scratch, you should make sure that you have everything needed.

It helps to list your family's favorites meals. Which recipes are you most fond of? If you are an organized person who has a weekly or monthly menu plan, you can take a look at it and figure out the ingredients that you use in a particular recipe. Multiplying the ingredients by 12 will give you an estimate of how many meals you'd make each month. This will help you determine how much food you need in your food cupboard.

Example: Rice and Vegetables

For a family of four, you will need two cups of rice and a can of mixed veggies. Multiply the rice by 12, (2 cups x12 = 24 cups of rice) for a full year. For 12 years, you will need 12 cans of vegetables. One pound is equivalent to approximately two cups of rice. For a family of four, you'd need 12 pounds rice if you used it only once per month to make one meal.

That is one way you can figure how much to store. But, it doesn't have to be that complicated. You can just use rough estimates and skip the math. This example illustrates how much food you need to feed your family for a single meal. It can be difficult to understand how 20 grocery stores are available to you when you need an ingredient for a meal. In a survival situation you only have what's in your pantry.

Don't forget to buy the little things like chocolate, coffee, and candy. While they are not essential for your survival, they help you feel normal. It is mental as well as physical to survive something catastrophic. You want to feel normal, and your kids should feel the same. If you spend every moment on edge and afraid, it won't do any good. A positive outlook is possible when you wake up, have your coffee, and plan your day.

Chapter 14: Preserving your Fresh Food

Learn how to preserve and store food, whether you are growing it yourself or buying it in bulk. This will save you a lot of money. Canning food doesn't need to be purchased at the grocery store. Canning food in the home allows you to have the freedom to choose the best fruits or vegetables for your family and keep it fresh without using preservatives.

For future growth, you'll want to begin growing your garden now. If there is a crisis in the future, you will need to be able to grow your food. There is a steep learning curve when gardening. If you don't have the time or the patience to do it right, it is worth it.

Canning

Canning vegetables and fruits is simple. You don't need any special equipment to can fruits and vegetables. There are many ways to learn how safe food can be preserved. The following supplies are necessary to get started with canning.

* Pressure Canner

* Mason jars

* Bands, lids

* Canning Tongs

* Funnel

* Strainer

* Pectin -- jams

* Vinegar and pickling spice for pickling

* Canning salt

You can find the best deals at your local farmer's market and local farms for bulk fruits, vegetables, and other produce. When possible, choose organic. While it may be more expensive, you will enjoy a better flavor and won't need to worry as much about pesticides.

Before canning, always sterilize the jars and lids. Failure to sterilize your jars, lids and bands before canning could lead to contamination. Your hard work may be put to waste. Food spoilage is caused by bacteria within sealed jars. Most extension offices and CDC recommend that home-canned food be stored for no more than 6 months to a calendar year. But, if it is properly stored and maintained, it can be extended for many years.

Canning doesn't necessarily have to be limited only to canning fruits, vegetables, and meat. There are many ways to create soup and stew mix that can be made ready to use with only a small amount of water. Imagine homemade chicken broth in a jar. While it will require some research and knowledge about food preservation, it is definitely worth it.

Dehydrating

It is another way to save money while building your survival food stock. A quality dehydrator will be a must-have investment. The Excalibur dehydrator is popular with preppers. It does the job well and it does it quickly. You can store dehydrated foods in mason-jars or use the Foodsaver to seal the food.

You can make jerky at home for a fraction the price of what you would pay in a grocery store. To create the perfect taste, experiment with different seasonings.

Mylar bags can be used for dehydrated foods. This is a great option because it keeps the food fresher and longer. Silica packs are great to put in your jars and bags along with your dehydrated goods. Molding can be caused by a lack of moisture removal.

Dehydration means that a large amount of water is removed from a food. Unfortunately, most nutrients are in the food's water or juices. You can snack on dehydrated food, but not enough to meet your daily calories. It lacks all the nutrients necessary to stay healthy.

Chapter 15: How to Replenish Your Food in a Survival Situation

If you don't have a long-term food supply, disaster can strike before you are prepared. This is not a problem if the natural disaster has only caused a temporary interruption to your food supply. Are you prepared for the worst? No. That is why you should prepare for anything.

Grow your own food to replenish your food source. This includes raising animals for their food. Chickens, rabbits, pigs, and other small animals are the easiest to raise. Cows are more difficult to rear and less prolific. You are better off investing in small animals.

It is best to have enough seeds in your arsenal to help you start your garden. Avoid buying the same seeds in every garden shop. You should only purchase heirloom seed.

Heirloom seeds must be used because they only produce vegetables with seeds that can easily be replanted. A $1 pack of seeds will not yield vegetables with more seeds than those sold elsewhere. The seed may sprout but it's unlikely to produce any edible vegetables. If you invest the extra money for heirloom seeds, it will ensure you have a source of food that is sustainable for many years.

Purchase in bulk, and then put the seeds in a refrigerator. If the power goes out and you don't have refrigeration, place your seeds somewhere cool to prevent them from sprouting.

Hunting

Learn how hunt. Even though you may not be keen on shooting Bambi, once you are hungry, it will become easier to hunt the deer. Either you choose to use a gun (or learn the basics of a bow & arrow), Make sure you have enough ammunition in case you decide to purchase a gun. Also, you can learn how to create traps and snares. This is a great method to hunt small game. It's okay to eat wild squirrels and other wildlife. You can make your food tasty with the spices and herbs you have stored or are growing.

Foraging

It is important to learn how you can forage. There are hundreds upon hundreds of edible wild plants. Even better, wild plants can be used medicinally. You will want to purchase a few books and learn as much as you can about this subject. You can't eat every plant you find. If you are unsure if a particular plant is safe to consume, follow these steps.

1. Rub a little bit of the herb on the inside and wrists. Let the plant sit for about 15-

30 minutes, then check to see whether there are any reactions. If you experience burning, redness or itching, the plant is toxic. If you do not feel any reaction, proceed to the next step.

2. Place a small part of the plant below your tongue. It is likely that you will immediately know if the plant is toxic. Wait between 15-30 minutes to test for reactions. If there are any symptoms such as burning or swelling of the tongue, or tingling sensations, it could be toxic. Move on to step 3.

3. Consume a portion. Wait 24 hours to see if you have any reactions. The signs of a negative reaction include diarrhea, vomiting, cramping and nausea. You can consume the plant with no side effects. You shouldn't overdo this.

Chapter 16: What is an electromagnetic pulse?

An electromagnetic pulse can be real and not fiction. It is real, and can be devastating for the places where it is performed. Chapter 2 will cover this in more detail. In the meantime you may be curious as to what exactly an electromagnetic impulse is.

An EMP simply means a sudden surge in electromagnetic radiation. This electromagnetic energy results from a rapid acceleration in supercharged electrons. Any device, appliance, and machine that is affected by this burst can then malfunction because the flow of energy used for its operation has been interrupted. EMP can also be described in electromagnetic spectrum. Energy is measured as hertz (Hz). Two elements make up the spectrum: frequency, or the number or distance between waves per second. Radio waves have low frequency, and wavelength. The frequency and wavelength of electromagnetic pulses, on the other side, are extremely high. They can often be measured in gigahertz.

You can think of the remote control on your TV as a microwave. How will the remote work in the microwave? The device will catch fire because the wiring and the chip inside the remote will be fried.

This is what happens in an EMP strike. The radiation energy from the microwave caused damage to the remote's electronics. EMP attacks are more dangerous than a microwave remote attack because the target does not need to be boxed in to launch the attack.

Lightning strikes is another common EMP attack example that you may not have heard of. Imagine sitting at home drinking beer and watching television on a rainy night. A lightning strike strikes a kilometer from your window, and suddenly you see it through the glass. Within seconds, your entire house has gone black. You rush to your basement and flip the switch to try to turn on the power again, but nothing. You are now subject to an EMP attack that manifests in the form lightning.

Although it may seem that the two examples are far apart enough to be considered EMP attacks you can still apply the science from the first example to the second. The lightning strike, which is the strongest manifestation of the electromagnetic pulse, is when supercharged particles are concentrated in such close quarters that they hit the target instantly. Similar to the second example, charged particles penetrate electrical components of any device and overwhelm them. Comparing these two examples, you can see that the former uses an unstable form of electromagnetic radiation which means that any object with an electrical component is susceptible to being attacked. The latter is a concentrated type of energy.

EMP attacks are more powerful than lightning strikes. They can be detected from as far away as 149,600,000. Solar flares is the third form of EMP. Solar flares are the result of high-energy, intense radiation from the sun's surface. Solar flares have such a powerful effect on radio transmissions that they can disrupt satellites and airwaves. A weakening signal on your television can result in static or striped images instead of the original broadcast. This is caused by the interference of the solar flare with the signal to the cable.

Before we go into more detail about the EMP, let's briefly review the history behind its discovery. In 1962, the United States created a nuclear bomb that was higher than the Soviet Union's. Operation Starfish Prime was named the mission. You should note that the closest human community was more than a thousand miles away. After the explosions, it was found that the electronics used to collect and analyze data malfunctioned. In Australia and California, radio transmissions were also reported as being interrupted. This led to the introduction of the electromagnetic pulse to the scientific community.

Researchers have divided the solar flares into three distinct categories based their wavelengths. First, we have X-class flares. This type emits more photons than any other and has the strongest wavelengths. X class flares can cause severe radio blackouts, and even damage to electronic devices. It emits a lot of radiation into the atmosphere. This has consequences for climate changes. One reason is that greenhouse gasses are trapped in the ozone. M-class flares, which cause short radio blackouts within the Earth's Polar Regions (Antarctica and Antarctica), are the second. C-class fares is a third category of minor flares, which are almost invisible and don't affect signals in comparison to the other two.

You might now wonder how artificial or natural EMP attacks are launched. EMP attacks are similar to the Cold War's experiments. An enormous radioactive aftershock will result from the explosion. This is different to a physical shockwave produced by the explosion. The radioactive aftershock may be more far reaching than the physical shockwave and may not feel as strong in the human body. It will, however, attack and overwhelm all electronic equipment in the affected area, depending upon the firepower and strength of the nuke.

On the other side, small-scale EMP weapons have undergone major improvements that do not employ nuclear warheads. These weapons are capable of emitting concentrated streams of electromagnetic radiation. A satellite dish mounted on the top of a vehicle is one such weapon. This combination is extremely deadly, as the EMP can strike multiple targets simultaneously in a short amount of time. This EMP weapon uses the same principle as the lightning strike but transmits the electromagnetic energy through the air.

In terms of distance covered, and projected energy, the portable EMP weapon has a lower power than a nuclear EMP. It is still a serious threat to the public. It is even more concerning that it has been reported to be used in the ongoing wars between the Middle East and Eastern Europe.

Don't believe that EMP attacks are over. Google searches will return hundreds of thousands results on how you can build your EMP transmitting devices. Even though these small-scale weapons only have the ability to destroy small devices like televisions, smartphones, and laptops they can also be used for other purposes. If you have the resources to make an EMP weapon that is more powerful, you can build one yourself. One video shows how a homemade EMP weapon can destroy a house within a radius of twenty yards. It's not necessary to be afraid if a terrorist group launches a nuclear weapon above us.

EMP attacks can happen from anywhere and at any hour.

Chapter 17: The Worst Case Scenario

One morning, you awaken. You hear cries outside your window. People panicking are visible, with plenty of food and valuables. You are left wondering what the heck is going on. You turn on the television, but it won't switch on. You plug it in. It is. You feel worried. You try to contact your friends but their phone is dead. You use your landline. It is also dead. At this point, everything in your home is dead. You run to the pantry and grab some supplies. Then you go to find your nearest friend. You gather all the supplies you need and pack it into your car. Unfortunately, your car doesn't start. You realize that everyone was carrying their stuff by foot. You panic as everyone else.

Then you see someone point up at the sky, and they say that a jet is rapidly descending. The plane is heading to your area. It travels at a speed one hundredth of a kilometer every second. In less than a second, it will crash into your area and kill everyone. It's obvious that you cannot escape the impact's reach. Your impending doom is realized and you fall to your knees praying to the higher power to explain what happened on that day when society was sent back into the Stone Age.

I don't think this is possible. As we discussed in Chapter 1 an EMP with sufficient power will knock out any power society has and basically send us back as before Benjamin Franklin flew the kite during storms.

In this scenario, the entire globe is affected by an EMP attack. It will last indefinitely. Because the effects of such an attack worldwide are numerous, we will only be able to discuss the implications for large cities and metropolitan areas. The list will provide you with some insight into how an EMP could impact those areas that are less modernized.

The most grave implication of an EMP strike on society is the disruption of the power grid. This would mean no electricity is generated and therefore, the population won't have access to utilities that use electricity. Everything in the world will look dark from a bird's-eye view. Light from lamps posts, signs and buildings, houses, etc. will not be available. People will have to turn to fire and battery-powered lighting as alternatives. To keep fires raging, people will turn to burning trash and cutting down forests to get light. This will only lead to a worsening effect on the planet's condition by releasing large amounts of carbon dioxide into our atmosphere.

Concerning batteries, people will need to have as many as possible batteries to power their devices. The panic buying that will result in chaos will create. This scenario will also include the theft of car batteries and mass cases of battery theft from supermarkets and grocery stores. Riots and other violent incidents are expected. Police and military forces will work together to protect society's mental health. But eventually, all batteries will run dry and people won't be able charge them. To meet their basic needs, the society will use gasoline and gasoline powered generators.

People will also be looting gasoline, in addition to batteries. This attack will be most likely to target gas stations. Similar to the mass looting batteries, authorities will try and control the crowds and prevent theft. But, keep in mind, these thieves are targeting large multinational gasoline suppliers. Not just any supermarket with four employees per shift. These multinationals have the financial resources to protect their assets, and they are aware of how expensive this commodity is. These corporations have their very own private security force that has the same firepower as National Guard. Private security has the right to kill anyone who tries to steal from them.

An altercation of greater proportions between multinational corporations, and the people will ensue. Both sides will make no concessions in their fight for survival. The battlefield where they will be fighting contains highly flammable liquid. One bullet could easily blow up an oil tanker. This would instantly bring down hundreds. But the combatants won't be deterred if they get what their hearts desire. This war will continue until the last drop is consumed of gasoline.

Attention multinationals and private security: Since there is no electricity, many security measures that depend on this will be deactivated immediately. Large institutions like banks, malls, or other large institutions that depend on increased security will be more easily hacked. These individuals will try to enter these establishments and steal valuable items. It will not be easy for thieves to break into these establishments.

EMP attacks could also affect security systems. Financial sector that relies on financial records to function will suffer severe consequences. The bank will lose all its money, and you won't be able to prove that it is yours. What happens next? This is how people get cash. The world is not dependent on money so this act is futile. However, many people believe that it does.

EMP attacks could also affect communications. Internet access, which is an integral part of every day life, will be unreachable. Social media will end. I don't know why but social media is no longer the best way to stay in touch with friends and family. It will be more difficult for people to communicate with those living at least a mile from them. These unpredicable situations will affect the emotions of many people, if they are not all. These will lead to rapid decisions, which will only cause more chaos for those concerned about their friends and families' lives.

EMP attacks in mid-air can be terrifying. EMP attack, which will immediately disable devices and gadgets, will also instantly destroy planes. When this happens, pilots, crew and passengers won't be able do anything. EMP attacks during mid-flight can result in death not only for those aboard, but also for anyone nearby.

As society continues using the last viable energy sources, the fight to secure food supplies will grow more desperate. This fight will begin from the day after the EMP attack. People will be able to hoard as much food, especially non-perishable items like canned goods or bottled water. People will initially empty out frozen foods before they go bad. These items are high in value due to their carbohydrate, fat and protein content. They are limited, and that is the most important thing. People will eventually run out of perishable foodstuffs and will then choose non-perishable food items. It is possible that they will also resort to animal killings or cannibalism.

Chapter 18: Surviving

Prevention is the best treatment, according to the old saying. EMP attacks are unpredictable and can be very dangerous. You can be prepared for anything by being prepared at any time. It is important to have enough supplies on hand. Also, remember to stockpile first aid supplies and bandages. These items are just the same as food or water.

This pantry will be used to store all these supplies. For three reasons, underground storage is a good idea.

First of all, it will be possible to build underground. Building underground is not restricted in terms of spatial dimensions. However, it's possible for neighbors to block your way.

Building underground will conceal your supplies from prying eyes and make it much easier to defend the storage space.

Underground construction offers a more secure way to access the area than building above it.

Finally, you could also use the underground space as a place to rest. This is similar with a nuclear bunker in which people can hide in the event of a bombing. As you can have some rest and are not afraid of being awakened again, an EMP bunker will greatly increase your chances for survival.

Similar to the above, you can make your storage area a faraday box. Faraday cells were designed to prevent static external and internal fields from reaching the enclosure. It is possible to save electronics and other devices by wrapping them in newspaper or plastic before storing them within the faraday enclosure.

Faraday enclosures can resist electromagnetic energy because of their design. This includes an aluminum foil-based conductive layer that is wrapped around the enclosure. This is done to protect electronic components from damage by the EMP attack.

First, the layers deflect the energy. Second, the layer absorbs energy via its conductive characteristics. The layer can also help create opposing forces. The faraday enclosure is made up of two sides. One side has negative electrons and the other is full of positive charges.

Newton's law explains that every force produces an equal and opposing reaction. This keeps electromagnetic energy out of the Faraday enclosure.

It is highly recommended that you install traps and security precautions, such as tripwires and improvised bomb devices that explode if unintentionally activated. These could be considered landmines.

These measures will significantly increase the protection for your territory.

Avoid electric vehicles as they are ineffective. This would include bikes, skateboards and skateboards. These transport options will allow you to travel much more quickly. You can even build a tuktuk-style bicycling system with a sidecar attached. It will make it easy to transport people or supplies from one point to the next.

www.ingramcontent.com/pod-product-compliance
Lightning Source LLC
Chambersburg PA
CBHW060501030426
42337CB00015B/1680